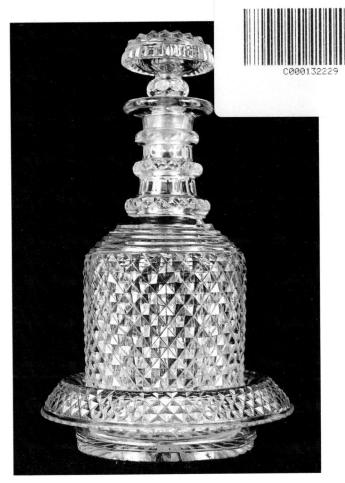

*A rare Regency diamond and prismatic cut decanter with original matching coaster. c.1820.*

# Decanters
## 1760-1930

David Leigh

A Shire book

Published in 2002 by Shire Publications Ltd,
Cromwell House, Church Street, Princes Risborough,
Buckinghamshire HP27 9AA, UK.
(Website: www.shirebooks.co.uk)

British Library Cataloguing in Publication Data:
Leigh, David
Decanters 1760-1930. – (Shire album; 411)
1. Decanters – History – 18th century
2. Decanters – History – 19th century
3. Decanters – History – 20th century
I. Title
748.8'2
ISBN 0 7478 0548 2

Cover: *A rare Victorian 'Tantalus' by Betjemanns, London. The gilt bronze frame is profusely chased with scrollwork and decorated around the base with flowers and foliage in red, blue, green and white enamel. The interior retains its original blue velvet and white silk linings. The original instruction label for using the patent locking mechanism is still pasted to the original red baize on the underside of the frame. The three square spirit decanters are cut all over in the 'brilliant' style and have lapidary stoppers. c.1880.*

ACKNOWLEDGEMENTS
The following are acknowledged for giving permission to use photographs of their decanters: Mr John Blakesley, Derbyshire; Christie's, London; Hanlin Gallery, Hong Kong; Mr Basil Loveridge; Mr David Powell, Oxford; and Sotheby's, London. All other photography is by David Leigh, courtesy of Laurie Leigh Antiques, Oxford.

Printed in Malta by Gutenberg Press Limited, Gudja Road,
Tarxien PLA 19, Malta.

# Contents

*A pair of Georgian plain tapered decanters, each dated 10th July 1797 on the front within an engraved cartouche. Each decanter is also engraved on the back with another cartouche enclosing the monogram 'EW'. With cut disc stoppers.*

# Foreword

This introduction to the development of the British decanter is primarily intended for those who might wish to collect decanters and would like to know more about them. Unfortunately, decanters made before the middle of the eighteenth century are now so scarce that they are seldom to be seen outside museums or famous collections. Consequently, this short survey begins around 1750, since it is still possible to encounter for sale examples from the second half of the eighteenth century. It is hoped that this history may help to illumine for the reader the obscurity that usually shrouds this neglected subject.

# The classic period
## 1760–1800

Above: *A Georgian slice-cut club-shaped decanter with a facet-cut 'Gothic' spire stopper. c.1765.*

Right: *A Georgian mallet-shaped decanter cut all over with hollow diamond facets and fitted with a 'Gothic' spire stopper. c.1770.*

In the late seventeenth century, the form of the decanter had been derived largely from that of the contemporary squat, short-necked wine bottle. By the end of the century the form had been refined into the *shaft and globe*, the body of the decanter becoming almost spherical and the neck more elongated. The shaft and globe decanter persisted into the middle of the eighteenth century, when it disappeared, only to be revived about a hundred years later in the Victorian era.

Around the middle of the eighteenth century the decanter began to find a life of its own. Two new forms were introduced that were not derived from the wine bottle: the narrow-shouldered or *mallet*-shaped decanter and the broad-shouldered or *club*-shaped decanter. The body of the mallet-shaped decanter, so called because of its resemblance to a stonemason's mallet, had narrow, sloping shoulders from which the sides of the decanter tapered *outwards* towards the base. By contrast, the club-shaped decanter, which resembled an Indian club, had broader shoulders and sides that tapered *inwards* towards the base. Both these types, which survived until the end of the century, were at first fitted with facet-cut 'Gothic' spire stoppers. Very soon, however, various forms of *cut disc* stopper, either circular or teardrop-shaped, were provided as alternatives. These stoppers would often have the edges of their flat surfaces cut with facets or hollow half-moons. Sometimes they would be scalloped around the edge. Later examples of the club-shaped decanter might sport the *lozenge* stopper, of which the otherwise plain teardrop-shaped finial was bevelled around the edge.

While the decanters of the first half of the eighteenth century had been fairly plain, various sorts of decoration began to manifest themselves on the mallet- and club-shaped decanters. One of the earliest styles of decoration consisted of flowers and foliage executed by a combination of rudimentary cutting and engraving: the stems and stalks were produced by engraved lines, while the leaves and petals of the flower heads comprised polished, round, hollow-cut facets. Another of the earliest forms of decoration covered the entire surface of

5

*Above left: A Georgian mallet-shaped decanter with a polished engraving of a large rose and foliage. With a cut disc stopper. c.1770.*

Above centre left: *A Georgian club-shaped decanter engraved with medallions and festoons of sprig and oval over cut hollow flutes. With a lozenge stopper. Probably Irish (Cork), c.1780.*

Above centre right: *A Georgian mallet-shaped decanter with a polished engraving of a rose, a closed bud and an opening bud. With a cut disc stopper. Possibly of Jacobite significance. c.1760.*

Above right: *A Georgian club-shaped decanter decorated with a slice-cut star beneath an arch supported by columns over hollow flutes. With a cut disc stopper. Possibly Irish (Waterford), c.1780.*

the decanter with shallow, hollow-cut diamond facets.

Decorative glass-cutting was in its infancy at this time, with the result that glasscutters were very conservative in their technique. Natural caution and fear of accidentally cutting right through the thickness of the glass led them to cut the surface of the glass at a very shallow angle. With this technique they produced festoons, stars and geometric patterns using broad, shallow, flat cuts. This type of cutting is characteristic of most of the second half of the eighteenth century and is popularly known as *slice* cutting. Slice cutting might be applied to the whole body of the decanter or, more frequently, might be used to make festoons and stars around the decanter's body. The shoulders of decanters were often slice-cut to complement hollow diamond facets cut to the neck. Narrow hollow comb flutes were sometimes cut around the base of mallet-shaped decanters, as were narrow zigzag mitre cuts.

By far the commonest form of decoration at this period was conventional wheel engraving. Various kinds of flowers and foliage as well as fruiting vines are the patterns most frequently encountered. Combinations of festoons, stars, flowers and vesicas are also to be seen. A less common decoration was the engraved wine label imitating the silver

*Far left: A Georgian tapered decanter engraved with flowers and foliage below hollow-cut diamond facets. With a cut disc stopper. c.1780.*

*Left: A Georgian blue tapered decanter with three triangular neck rings and a matching lozenge stopper. Probably Belfast, c.1790.*

wine labels introduced towards the end of the first half of the eighteenth century. The name of the intended wine, which might be *claret, white wine, champagne*, or so on, would be engraved inside a label-shaped cartouche that would appear to be suspended from the neck of the decanter by an engraved chain. Fruiting vines would often surround the label or, occasionally, hops and barley if the decanter were intended for ale or beer. Not unnaturally, these decanters are known as *labelled* decanters.

In the 1770s another decanter shape was introduced that was a modification of the mallet-shaped decanter. The base was narrower with a taller body that tapered inwards towards the neck without any discernible shoulder. This became known as the *tapered* decanter. Unlike the mallet- and club-shaped decanters, the tapered decanter was usually made with a narrow lip. The more delicate style of this decanter meant that any cut decoration tended to be fairly discreet, preference being given to engraving. It might be provided with either the cut disc or the lozenge stopper. In the 1790s, the tapered decanter was occasionally made with two or three neck rings for added finger grip. This feature is often to be observed on tapered decanters made in Ireland.

The earliest English decanters, such as those by the inventor of lead crystal, George Ravenscroft, and his successor, Hawley Bishopp, were provided with loose-fitting stoppers, often more like lids. Until the middle of the eighteenth century, stoppers were usually not fitted at all. The stopper peg was usually blown somewhat undersized to allow it to drop without difficulty into the

*Far left: A rare Georgian tapered decanter with five flat neck rings and a cut disc stopper. Probably Belfast, c.1790.*

*Left: A Georgian tapered decanter engraved with flowers and foliage above basal moulded flutes. With a moulded target stopper. Belfast, c.1790.*

neck of the decanter and hang there. The reason for this imprecision was that although grinding pastes, which allow the stopper to be ground into the neck's aperture, are mentioned as early as 1675, they did not seem to come into general use until the middle of the eighteenth century. Even as late as the early nineteenth century many Irish decanters, particularly those from Belfast, were made and supplied with their stoppers not ground to fit. The introduction of coarse grinding pastes allowed the stopper to be fitted more carefully. Since the process was carried out by hand and required a certain amount of guesswork, the fit was often still less than perfect. The frequently poor fitting of stoppers does not seem to have particularly troubled the Georgian owners of decanters. This method of fitting stoppers left the peg and the interior of the top of the neck with a roughened, grey surface, the effect of which can be observed on most Georgian decanters made before 1820. However, determining the date when grinding pastes came into general use is complicated by the probability that many loose-fitting stoppers were ground in at a later date to improve their fit.

Towards the end of the eighteenth century yet another new decanter shape was introduced. The body was roughly barrel-shaped while the neck typically had three neck rings of a variety of profiles (round, triangular, annular, feathered, flat) and a pronounced lip. Contemporary advertisements sometimes refer to this new style as *Prussian*, although nowadays it is more usually called *barrel*-shaped. One of two forms of stopper was usually fitted to it. The first was yet another variant of the cut disc stopper: the thick circular finial was bevelled around the edge and cut on both sides with a *lenticle* or lens. This is known as the *target* stopper, although it has acquired the popular nickname of 'bull's eye'. The second form of stopper was an entirely new type and consisted of an umbrella-shaped finial on a straight stem. Since it strongly resembles a mushroom, it is known as the *mushroom* stopper. Early examples were usually cut with

*Below: A pair of plain Georgian barrel-shaped decanters with three plain neck rings and star-cut mushroom stoppers. c.1800.*

Left: *A Georgian plain straight-sided decanter with three plain neck rings, the body engraved with an emblazoned label for 'PORT'. With a target stopper. c.1800.*

Right: *A Georgian barrel-shaped decanter with two feathered neck rings and basal moulded flutes. The disc stopper has vertical and horizontal moulded ridges, but note that the stopper has never been fitted. Belfast, c.1800.*

Far right: *An unusual Georgian barrel-shaped decanter with two annular neck rings and two annular bands to the body. With a target stopper. Probably Irish (Cork), c.1800.*

Below left: *A Georgian tapered decanter engraved with zigzags, stars and ovals. With a lozenge stopper. c.1780.*

Below right: *A pair of plain Georgian barrel-shaped decanters with three plain neck rings and target stoppers. c.1800.*

9

Right: *A Georgian mallet-shaped decanter, the neck cut with hollow diamond facets above slice cutting to the shoulder over basal hollow flutes and 'printies'. With a cut disc stopper. c.1770.*

Far right: *An Irish Georgian mallet-shaped decanter engraved with wavy lines over festoons, bows and foliage above basal moulded flutes. With a moulded ribbed target stopper. Probably Cork, c.1800.*

Left: *A Georgian barrel-shaped decanter with three plain neck rings, the body engraved with fruiting vines. With a target stopper. c.1800.*

a simple multi-pointed star. At this period the body of the barrel decanter would be either plain or discreetly decorated with wheel engraving or shallow cutting. In Ireland, the barrel-shaped decanter would often be decorated with a row of narrow moulded basal flutes. The two types of stopper provided for the Irish tapered decanter were also used for the Irish barrel-shaped decanter: the *moulded* disc stopper, which could be either plain or decorated with vertical and horizontal moulded ridges, or the *moulded* target stopper, which

*A pair of Georgian labelled blue tapered decanters with gilded fancy labels for 'SHERRY' and 'PORT' suspended by chains, in imitation of typical contemporary silver wine labels. With original blue lozenge stoppers. c.1790.*

usually had small flutes moulded into the bevels around the lenticle on each side. In addition to these, the *moulded* mushroom stopper was also used.

The barrel-shaped decanter was destined to have a long life. It underwent a number of transformations that allowed it to survive in various forms for several decades before finally disappearing around the middle of the nineteenth century.

# From restraint to exuberance
## 1800–1830

*A rare Irish decanter with three feathered neck rings and moulded basal flutes. With a moulded target stopper (unfitted). The base is embossed 'WATERLOO C⁰ CORK'. c.1820.*

The barrel-shaped decanter, introduced in the late eighteenth century, was the dominant decanter form throughout the late Georgian and Regency periods. Cutting rather than engraving became the favoured type of decoration. At first, cutting remained fairly simple, combining broad shoulder flutes with narrow basal comb flutes. To these were often added rows, bands or reserves of relief diamonds. The plain pyramidal *relief* diamond had begun to appear in the years before 1800 and became an increasingly popular decorative feature. In the early nineteenth century three new kinds of diamond cutting were added to the repertoire: the *strawberry* diamond, the *hobnail* diamond and the *cross-cut* diamond. The relief diamond and the strawberry diamond were to dominate glass-cutting throughout this period. At first these elements were used with some restraint. However, the gradual replacement in the glasshouses of hand- or treadle-operated cutting wheels by more powerful steam-driven cutting wheels encouraged cutters to become ever bolder and more inventive. Cutting became not only deeper but also more elaborate, using prisms and swirls, as well as vertical and slanted blazes and circular lenticles or 'printies'. To allow for this, glassblowers gradually increased the thickness of the sides of the decanter, thus greatly adding to its weight. Neck rings were often cut with diamonds or facets. Horizontal and vertical prismatic cutting increasingly came to be combined with strawberry, hobnail or relief diamonds in the 1820s, when it was not uncommon for the entire surface of the decanter to be cut. A large multi-pointed star was often cut into the base of the decanter to hide any trace of the pontil mark. At this time, neck rings were frequently discarded in favour of horizontal prismatic cutting extending from the shoulder to the lip. In the 1820s there was a tendency to straighten the sides of the decanter so that it became quite cylindrical. This new variant co-existed with the more bulbous curved barrel form. This decade also gave rise to one further form of cut decoration that became very fashionable: the rounded cut pillar flute. The technique of producing this convex fluting or 'reeding' on glass using flat-profiled cutting wheels was difficult, time-consuming and, consequently, expensive. Although pillar flutes were usually cut vertically, some rare instances of horizontally

*A rare Irish decanter cut with alternating panels of sunbursts and diamonds below broad shoulder flutes and three annular neck rings. With original matching hollow-blown stopper. Cork, c.1820.*

Above left: *An Irish ship's decanter, the neck cut with three flat rings and broad flutes over broad shoulder flutes and narrow hollow basal flutes. With a star-cut mushroom stopper. Cork, c.1810.*

Above centre: *An Irish ship's decanter with three triangular neck rings over broad shoulder flutes and narrow hollow basal flutes. With a target stopper. Probably Belfast, c.1810.*

Above right: *A ship's decanter with four plain neck rings over broad shoulder flutes and narrow hollow basal flutes. With a star-cut mushroom stopper. c.1810.*

*A pair of Georgian decanters, each with one plain and two diamond-cut neck rings, the bodies cut with a broad band of strawberry diamonds over a row of lenticles or 'printies', diagonal mitre cuts and fine diamonds. The matching stoppers are cut with strawberry diamonds. c.1820.*

13

cut ones have been observed. All of the decorative devices described above were used both by the English glasshouses and by the Irish glasshouses at Waterford and Cork.

Although at first the target stopper continued to be used as an alternative to the mushroom stopper on the more simply cut barrel-shaped decanters, the mushroom stopper became almost a *sine qua non* for the more elaborately cut ones. Very occasionally, instead of being cut with a star, the mushroom stopper was cut to match the body of the decanter. The original pronounced umbrella profile of the mushroom finial gradually gave way to one that was flatter and thicker. As the profusion and elaboration of the cut decoration increased the heaviness of the decanter's appearance, the finial of the mushroom stopper was sometimes blown hollow so that it formed a flattened sphere. Solid or hollow ball stoppers are also encountered occasionally. Both the flattened hollow-blown stopper and the ball stopper were always cut to match the decoration on the body of the decanter. Whether it was at the

*An elaborate Regency decanter with three diamond-cut neck rings over broad shoulder flutes and a band of diamonds above teardrop- and vesica-shaped reserves of diamonds. With a matching diamond- and star-cut ball stopper. c.1820.*

*A Regency decanter with three plain neck rings over horizontal prisms, a broad wavy band of diamonds and basal comb flutes. With a star-cut mushroom stopper. c.1820.*

*Far left: A pair of Regency decanters cut with horizontal prisms over a broad band of diamonds above a row of pillar flutes. With matching pillar-fluted and diamond-cut hollow-blown mushroom stoppers. c.1820*

*Left: A straight-sided Regency decanter with one plain and two diamond-cut neck rings over horizontal prisms, a row of vertical mitre flutes and a broad band of diamonds. With a matching diamond- and mitre-cut mushroom stopper. c.1820.*

Above: left: *A Georgian decanter with three plain neck rings above broad shoulder flutes and narrow basal hollow comb flutes. With a star-cut mushroom stopper. c.1810.*

Above centre: *A Georgian decanter with three plain neck rings over broad shoulder flutes and a band of large strawberry diamonds and prisms above basal broad flutes. With a star-cut mushroom stopper. c.1820.*

Above right: *A Georgian decanter with three plain neck rings over broad shoulder flutes and festoons of vertical blazes enclosing strawberry-cut reserves above basal broad flutes. With a star-cut mushroom stopper. c.1820.*

Above left: *A pair of Regency decanters with three annular collars over broad shoulder flutes and a band of diamonds above Gothic arch-shaped reserves of diamonds over basal mitre flutes. With matching diamond-cut mushroom stoppers. Probably Cork, 1820.*

Above right: *A pair of Regency decanters with horizontal prisms cut to the neck and shoulder over strawberry diamonds. With star-cut mushroom stoppers. c.1820.*

*A Regency decanter with prismatic cutting to the neck above swirls of fine diamonds, each terminating with a lenticle, over prisms and broad basal flutes. With a matching mushroom stopper. Perrin Geddes, Warrington, c.1820.*

*A rare Royal straight-sided decanter cut with horizontal prisms to the neck over broad shoulder flutes and vertical prisms. The body of the decanter is set with a sulphide of a crest or badge for a brother of King George IV depicting a crowned lion standing on a coronet, enclosed in the Garter carrying the motto 'HONI SOIT QUI MAL Y PENSE' and surmounted by a coronet. Apsley Pellatt, London, c.1825.*

*A Regency decanter with two plain neck rings over broad shoulder flutes, a band of diamonds and swirls of fine diamonds, each terminating in a lenticle. With a matching diamond- and star-cut ball stopper. c.1820.*

instigation of the customer or of the glassmaker, it came to be felt that the roughened grey surfaces of the stopper peg and the top of the neck produced by the fitting process spoiled the fine appearance of these elaborately cut Regency pieces. Consequently, after 1820 (although earlier examples are sometimes seen) it gradually became standard practice to polish bright these rough grey surfaces to remove all evidence of the grinding.

The Regency period gave rise to glass-cutting of extraordinary innovation and invention. The exuberance and technical virtuosity of Regency cut decoration has rarely, if ever, been surpassed.

*A very rare example of a straight-sided diamond-cut Regency decanter, with one plain and two diamond-cut neck rings, with its original diamond-cut coaster with a turnover rim. With a matching diamond- and mitre-cut mushroom stopper. c.1820.*

# Transition: William IV to Victoria
## 1830–1850

The two decades of the 1830s and 1840s represent a transition from the Regency to the early Victorian period. Inspiration continued to be derived from the forms established earlier in the century. However, although the true barrel-shaped decanter was largely superseded by its cylindrical cousin, two new variants were introduced at this time. In the first, the outward curve of the body was retained but the neck was given a sharp inward curve, so that the entire profile of the decanter was decidedly 'S' shaped. A single large ring was applied to the base of the neck and the whole decanter was usually cut with six or eight broad flutes. Typically a tall, hollow-blown fluted spire stopper was fitted. This type of decanter was known as *fancy*-shaped. The second new variant was based on the cylindrical decanter except that the sides tapered inwards towards the base. Either one or three rings would be applied to the neck, which would be fitted either with a hollow-blown fluted spire stopper or a heavy round or octagonal mushroom stopper. The round mushroom stopper would be flat and cut with a six- or eight-pointed star, while the octagonal version would be cut with facets. This type of decanter would also normally be cut with broad flutes. The type with one neck ring was known as the *Nelson*, while that with three neck rings was known as the *Royal*. The reason for these names remains obscure. The Nelson decanter also appears in a narrower, more bottle-shaped version.

While the broad-fluted style described above was evidently popular during this transitional period, some of the decorative features used in the 1820s continued to be used on some of the more elaborately cut pieces. However, glassmakers increasingly eschewed the exuberant detail of the Regency for a plainer style based on ever bolder and deeper cutting. Wide, deep mitre cuts would often mark out Gothic arches. The fields contained within these arches might be left plain, or they might be given domed or convex forms

*A rare William IV smoky-blue decanter cut all over with broad flutes, the neck cut across with fine prisms, the body with a broad plain band cut in relief. With a matching octagonal facet-cut mushroom stopper. c.1835.*

*A William IV 'Nelson' decanter, the neck cut with a row of short flutes over a plain ring above broad shoulder flutes and vertical mitre flutes. With a fluted hollow-blown spire stopper. c.1835.*

using the techniques developed for making pillar flutes. Another very expensive style required the decanter to be very thickly blown and then tiers of rounded arches or festoons would be cut around the body of the decanter. These arches or festoons were usually produced by convex cutting, although sometimes this was combined with some concave cutting to increase the three-dimensional impression. The sculptured look of pieces cut in this way produced an effect of heaviness, even of lumpiness, abandoning the elegant brilliance of the previous decades. Such was the depth of the diamond cutting on some of the pieces shown at the Great Exhibition of 1851 that some critics described them as 'prickly monstrosities'.

While coloured glass, particularly blue, green and amethyst, had occasionally been used for decanters in the late eighteenth and early nineteenth century, it seems to have fallen into disuse during the Regency period. In the 1840s coloured decanters

*A pair of early Victorian apple-green decanters, the broad-fluted necks with a single facet-cut ring, the bodies cut in Gothic arches. With matching hollow-blown fluted spire stoppers. Richardsons, Stourbridge, c.1840.*

19

*An early Victorian green-cased decanter cut with broad flutes above and below the neck ring over arched panels with large lenticles. With a matching green-cased hollow-blown stopper. c.1840.*

once again began to appear. New colours were invented, such as topaz yellow, apple green and peacock blue. The stage was now set for the profusion of new colours and decorative techniques that were to be developed during the Victorian era.

# The Victorian era
## 1850–1900

A complete change of style occurred about the midpoint of the nineteenth century. For inspiration Victorian glassmakers looked back to the early eighteenth century, to a form that had been defunct for a hundred years.

The shape that attracted the attention of the Victorians was the venerable *shaft and globe*, new examples of which were shown at the Great Exhibition of 1851. This shape was to dominate decanter making for the rest of the century. In its classic form, the body of the shaft and globe decanter was fairly spherical, but in later examples it was somewhat flattened. In the 1860s the growing interest in classicism led glassmakers to look to another historical form for inspiration, this time the ancient Greek *amphora*. The lightly blown amphora-shaped decanter had an ovoid body on a flat foot and a neck that was shorter than that of the shaft and globe. Frequently Victorian glassmakers even reproduced the Grecian *trefoil* lip. This graceful decanter became the principal alternative to the shaft and globe. Another old form that was revived occasionally in the late nineteenth century was the mallet-shaped decanter.

Although a large number of stopper shapes were used in the Victorian era, one basic principle applied. Victorian decanters would be fitted either with a hollow-blown stopper that would always be decorated to match the decanter, or with the increasingly fashionable solid, facet-cut *lapidary* stopper. Victorian technology allowed for great improvements in the fitting of stoppers. A *reamer* fitted to a lathe was used to give a precise interior taper to the neck of the decanter, while a *die* was used to reproduce the same taper on the peg of the stopper. Provided that the ground surfaces were not over-polished, the result was a perfect fit.

Above: *A Victorian shaft and globe decanter cut with hollow hexagonal facets above a row of 'printies' over flat diamonds. With a matching hollow-blown stopper. c.1880.*

To prevent the stoppers being muddled up, the Victorian *stopperer*, whose job was to fit the stoppers into the decanters, often inscribed with a diamond point a number on both the stopper and the decanter. These numbers are very small and can be quite difficult to find. On the stopper, the number can be found on the base of the neck, on the side of the peg or on the base of the peg. On the decanter, the number can be found just inside the top of the neck where it joins the lip, on the top surface of the lip, on

Right: *A Victorian shaft and globe decanter, the neck cut with notched broad flutes over engraved panels of foliage and vertical stripes and a band of cut hobnails. With a matching cut and engraved stopper. c.1870*

Above left: *A Victorian shaft and globe decanter cut with hollow diamond facets over finely etched flowers and foliage. The matching stopper is cut with hollow diamond facets. Probably etched by John Northwood, Wordsley, c.1880.*

Above centre: *A Victorian ruby-cased shaft and globe decanter cut with large 'printies'. The matching ruby-cased stopper is also cut with 'printies'. c.1880.*

Above right: *A pair of Victorian decanters, each cut with notched broad flutes over panels of diamonds enclosing four raised reserves engraved alternately with flowers and foliage, and fruiting vines. Both with fluted stoppers. c.1880.*

Above left: *A pair of Victorian footed shaft and globe decanters with trefoil lips, very finely etched with panels containing different kinds of birds in foliage. With matching hollow-blown etched stoppers. Etched by John Northwood, Wordsley, c.1865.*

Above right: *A pair of Victorian shaft and globe decanters cut with broad flutes above two kinds of finely etched ferns. With hollow-blown fluted stoppers. c.1880.*

*Right: A rare Victorian white-trailed ruby-cased amphora-shaped decanter, with a clear neck ring and foot and a matching stopper. c.1860.*

*Far right: A Victorian amphora-shaped decanter cut with notched broad flutes above diagonal panels of hobnail diamonds and pillar flutes. The scalloped foot is cut with hobnail diamonds. With a matching stopper. Stevens & Williams, Stourbridge, c.1880.*

*Below: A Victorian decanter cut with broad flutes over three panels, each finely engraved with a different kind of fern. With a matching engraved stopper. c.1875.*

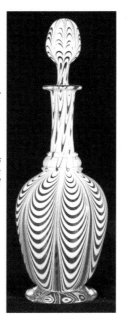

*Right: A Victorian amphora-shaped decanter cut all over in the 'Russian' pattern below hollow-cut hexagonal facets. With a matching cut stopper with facet-cut collar. c.1890.*

the edge of the lip, on the lip's underside, or even at the top of the outside of the neck immediately beneath the lip. In rare instances it has even been found on the base of the decanter. The Victorian stopperer did not always number his work and, in the case of pairs, did not always number both decanters. Where both halves of a pair of decanters are numbered, the numbers need not be consecutive. The numbers merely reflect the order in which the stoppers were fitted.

The complex patterns devised by Regency glasscutters were now abandoned in favour of bolder and simpler styles. The shaft and globe decanter was often cut with oval lenticles or 'printies', sometimes in combination with bands of flat diamonds or other devices produced by bold mitre cutting. Fields of fine diamonds also appear. Wheel engraving was sometimes combined with cutting or used alone. The neck of the decanter might be cut with broad flutes, sometimes with notching, or with hollow diamond or hexagonal facets. In the 1880s an elaborate geometric style of cutting based on straight-line mitre cuts was imported from the United States. It became known as the *brilliant* style and the plain or star-cut octagonal hobnail was a notable feature. Its most extravagant manifestation was the so-called *Russian* pattern, originally made for the Russian ambassador to Washington in 1882. This very

Above left:  *A Victorian shaft and globe decanter cut with alternate horizontal bands of cross-cut diamonds and pillar flutes over vertical pillar flutes and bands of cross-cut diamonds. With a matching stopper. Probably Stevens & Williams, c.1880.*

Above right: *A Victorian 'rock crystal' amphora-shaped decanter on a scalloped foot with a deep polished engraving of orchids and foliage over swirling plume pillars. With a matching hollow-blown stopper. Stevens & Williams, c.1880.*

expensive, deeply cut pattern was very soon reproduced by some of the great glasshouses in Stourbridge. In the last decades of the century, the public's desire for reproductions of historical styles of glass led to a revival of some of the old Regency cutting patterns. These were used not only on copies of Regency decanters but elements from these patterns were mixed with those of more conventional Victorian styles.

Above left: *A Victorian decanter cut in the 'brilliant' style on a star-cut foot. With a matching brilliant-cut stopper. c.1880.*

Above centre: *A Victorian tapered ruby-cased decanter decorated in intaglio with a herringbone pattern. With a matching ruby-cased stopper. Stevens & Williams, Stourbridge, c.1895.*

Above right: *A Victorian amphora-shaped decanter cut all over with diamonds below notched broad flutes. With a lapidary stopper. Stevens & Williams, Stourbridge, c.1880.*

Right: *A pair of Victorian amphora-shaped decanters cut with large swirling mitre flutes below bands of cut hobnails. On domed and scalloped star-cut feet and with lapidary stoppers. c.1890.*

Far left: *A Victorian decanter, double-cased with ruby over amber over clear glass, engraved all over with fruiting vines. With a matching stopper. Stevens & Williams, c.1900.*

Left: *A Victorian amphora-shaped decanter cut with marquise-shaped reserves of herringbone. c.1880.*

Left: *A Victorian shaft and globe decanter with all-over white trailing and a clear neck ring and foot. With a matching white-trailed stopper. c.1860.*

Coinciding with the introduction of the amphora-shaped decanter in the 1860s was the rise of the Aesthetic movement. Encouraged by the art critic John Ruskin, who declared all cut glass to be 'barbarous', the followers of fashion avoided cut glass, preferring to have their glass decorated with delicate engraving or acid etching. The classical amphora-shaped decanter was their preferred choice. Acid etching, developed largely by John Northwood, probably the most important Victorian glass decorator, became a very fashionable alternative to wheel engraving. In the 1860s, fashionable aestheticism particularly favoured classical motifs such as the key pattern, the anthemion and even classical figures and scenes often derived from the works of John Flaxman. More naturalistic ornament was also in vogue. In particular, fern decoration, inspired by a book on ferns published in the late 1850s, became exceedingly popular during the second half of the nineteenth century.

The success of the Venetian glass exhibits at the Great

Far right: *A Victorian brilliant-cut flagon-shaped decanter with broad flutes over hobnails. With a pointed lapidary stopper. c.1890.*

Right: *A Victorian amber amphora-shaped decanter cut with hollow hexagonal facets over a row of stars and ovals above flat diamonds. With a matching hollow-blown diamond-cut stopper. c.1880.*

Right: *A Victorian decanter cut with hollow hexagonal facets over large diamonds and prisms. With a star-cut foot and a matching diamond- and prismatic-cut stopper. By Stevens & Williams, Stourbridge, c.1890.*

Exhibition led to a vogue for reproductions of early Venetian glass. By the 1870s some British glassmakers, such as James Powell, had begun to incorporate Venetian techniques into simpler, more modern styles using subtle ribbing, dimpling and pincer-worked decoration. Followers of the Arts and Crafts movement favoured this nineteenth-century *façon de Venise*.

The Victorian fascination with science and technology led Victorian glassmakers to experiment with all kinds of minerals to produce new colours of glass. The more expensive, coloured decanters were produced by *casing*, where coloured glass was overlaid on clear glass. The coloured layer would then be cut through to reveal the clear layer. Very occasionally, several layers of different colours were used. Cutting at different depths would reveal each of the different colours.

In the late 1870s a new and very expensive form of decoration was introduced. The very thickly blown glass was laboriously sculpted into lobes by use of the cutting or engraving wheel. The surface of the glass would then be covered with deep engraving in a variety of styles, from classical scrollwork to dense,

Above left: *A pair of Victorian shaft and globe decanters cut with broad flutes over cross-cut diamonds and narrow vertical mitre flutes. With lapidary stoppers. c.1890.*

Above right: *A pair of Victorian mallet-shaped decanters cut with hollow diamond facets above a broad band of notched vertical mitre flutes between horizontal bands of brilliant cutting. With a matching hollow-blown stopper. c.1870.*

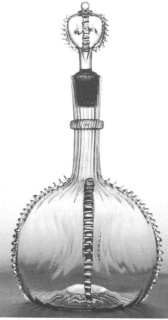

Far left: *A rare Victorian four-sided dimpled decanter with subtle vertical moulded ribbing. A feathered ring is applied to the neck and pincer-worked edging is applied to each of the four corners. With a pincer-worked heart-shaped stopper. James Powell & Sons, Whitefriars, London, c.1870.*

Left: *A rare Victorian four-sided dimpled decanter with subtle vertical moulded ribbing. Again, a feathered ring is applied to the neck and pincer-worked edging is applied to each of the four corners. With a matching hollow-blown four-sided dimpled stopper. James Powell & Sons, Whitefriars, London, c.1880.*

*A rare Victorian bellows-shaped decanter with subtle vertical moulded ribbing and spiral trailing to the neck. The spirally trailed spire stopper has pincer-worked edges. James Powell & Sons, Whitefriars, London, c.1890.*

naturalistic representations of marine life. The whole surface would then be acid polished to make all the decoration bright. The effect was to make pieces treated in this way look like carved rock crystal. This style, consequently, is known as *rock crystal* engraving. Rock crystal engraved pieces of the 1880s tended to be rather heavy and elaborate in appearance. Production was small, very labour intensive and extremely costly.

Around 1890, John Northwood devised a new technique that would produce a similar effect to rock crystal engraving but at a much lower cost. This technique, known as *intaglio*, used a specially designed, very small cutting wheel called a 'tag' wheel. This produced deep, crisp engraving that was polished bright, as in rock crystal engraving. Pieces decorated in intaglio were more lightly blown and the surface of the glass was not usually sculpted or lobed. Intaglio could also be combined with other types of decoration, such as wheel engraving, acid etching or conventional cutting. It was also used on rock crystal engraved pieces in the 1890s although, on the whole, heavy 'rock crystal' was less fashionable in this decade. The introduction of intaglio and new developments in rock crystal technique proved particularly apposite for the new artistic style that made its appearance at the end of the nineteenth century, the *Art Nouveau*.

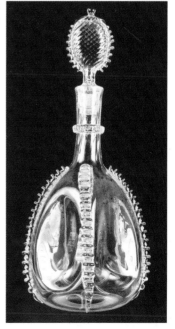

*A rare Victorian four-sided dimpled decanter with subtle vertical moulded ribbing. A feathered ring is applied to the neck and pincer-worked edging is applied to each of the four corners. The elaborate hollow-blown spire stopper has diagonal trailing and pincer-worked edges. James Powell & Sons, Whitefriars, London, c.1870.*

# From Art Nouveau to Art Deco
## 1900–1930

Towards 1900 a lighter style of 'rock crystal' was introduced. The glass was blown much thinner, the lobes being produced by moulding rather than sculpting. These moulded lobes were then sharpened by finely cut outlines. The favoured styles of polished engraving used on these pieces were derived from the late eighteenth century.

The new artistic fashion that appeared at this time, the Art Nouveau, was important for the effect it had on both the form and the decoration of the decanter. Interest in nature led glassmakers to design shapes and styles of decoration that were both fluid and full of movement. The use of moulded spiral or writhen ribbing was particularly fashionable and was often combined with dimpling. However, more conventional decorative techniques were also adapted and applied to these Art Nouveau shapes. While Art Nouveau glass was adopted by the fashionable *avant garde*, the bulk of glass produced at this time followed the styles established during the late Victorian period.

The intervention of the First World War between 1914 and 1918 was to have a profound effect on glassmaking. The trauma of four years of war produced a dramatic change in the nation's mood. The straitened post-war economic climate caused a major change in the operation of the glasshouses. They were gradually forced to abandon making glass for individual customers, in favour of producing glass on a mass scale to sell through retail outlets in the high street. The expensive, labour-intensive styles such as rock crystal were largely abandoned, except to special order. The conditions were ripe for the arrival of a new simple style that began to make its appearance in the early 1920s. This new style was heavily featured at the *Exposition des Arts Décoratives et Industrielles Modernes* that took place in Paris in 1925. Such was the success of this exhibition that it gave its abbreviated name to this style, which became known as *Art Deco*. The Art Deco style rapidly began to influence the design of everything from typography to architecture and dominated fashion through the 1920s and 1930s. Art Deco glass was

Above: *An Edwardian Art Nouveau decanter cut with large strawberry diamonds over vertical hollow flutes. c.1910.*

Above right: *An Edwardian Art Nouveau waisted decanter decorated in intaglio with a quatrefoil stopper. Thomas Webb & Sons, Stourbridge, c.1910.*

Left: *An Edwardian 'rock crystal' style decanter engraved with festoons and bows over pillar flutes. Thomas Webb & Sons, Stourbridge, c.1910.*

*Above left: An Edwardian Art Nouveau dimpled decanter with subtle spiral ribbing and a feathered double ring to the neck. With a matching hollow-blown spirally ribbed and dimpled stopper. James Powell & Sons, Whitefriars, London, c.1900.*

*Above centre left: An Edwardian helmet-shaped decanter decorated all over in intaglio with flowers, foliage, scrollwork and Gothic arches. With a matching hollow-blown stopper decorated in intaglio. c.1910.*

*Above centre right: An Edwardian 'rock crystal' style gourd-shaped decanter decorated in intaglio with festoons of foliage, flowers and ribbons, over basal plume pillars. Thomas Webb & Sons, Stourbridge, c.1910.*

*Above right: An amphora-shaped decanter decorated in intaglio with an oriental scene depicting fishermen in junks, houses, trees and birds over cut flat diamonds. With a matching hollow-blown diamond-cut stopper. Probably Stevens & Williams, Stourbridge, c.1920.*

characterised by clean, simple lines, frequently based on geometric shapes. Decoration was kept to a minimum, the preference being for cutting or intaglio work that used straight lines, curves or horizontal bands. Decanters in clear glass might be enhanced by coloured stoppers, often in amber, opaque white or black.

The natural conservatism of the British meant that less Art Deco style glass was produced in Great Britain than on the Continent. As was the case with Art Nouveau, Art Deco tended to be patronised by those most interested in the latest fashions, most people preferring glass of a more traditional design. The application of some of the older patterns of cutting to the new Art Deco shapes was a typical British compromise to give Art Deco a wider appeal. Unfortunately, Art Deco glass came to an abrupt end in Britain with the outbreak of the Second World War in 1939. When not requisitioned by the Government for war work, the glasshouses were required by government regulation to produce only 'utility' wares. The situation in Europe was different. The German economy remained on a peacetime footing until almost the middle of the war. Both in Germany

Far left: *An Art Deco conical decanter cut with broad flutes to the neck. With an open-topped conical amber stopper in the form of a wine glass. Stuart & Sons, Stourbridge, c.1935.*

Left: *An Art Deco ovoid decanter decorated with cut leaves and ferns below broad flutes and horizontal prisms. With a solid fluted stopper. Stuart & Sons, Stourbridge, c.1930.*

and in the countries that were under German control, the glasshouses continued to make fashionable products for the domestic market until the German economy and war machine began to disintegrate around 1944. The gradual economic recovery that began to take place in Great Britain and Europe around 1950 coincided with a change of taste. Designers regarded Art Deco as a pre-war style. It was abandoned and remained entirely out of favour for half a century until it returned to fashion in the 1990s.

Below left: *An Art Deco conical decanter decorated in intaglio below cut broad flutes. With a matching hollow-blown stopper. Stuart & Sons, Stourbridge, c.1935.*

Below centre: *An Art Deco ovoid decanter decorated in intaglio with stylised leaves. With a solid fluted stopper. Stuart & Sons, Stourbridge, c.1930.*

Left: *An Art Deco conical decanter with subtle moulded spiral ribbing and decorated with a band of fine 'brilliant' style cutting. With a matching hollow-blown spirally ribbed stopper. Thomas Webb & Sons, Stourbridge, c.1925.*

# Claret jugs, wine ewers and carafes

*Claret jug* is a universally used popular name for a decanter with a handle. Its form is that of a decanter of conventional shape for its period but with the addition of a handle and a pouring lip. It is almost invariably fitted with a stopper. The origin of the name is uncertain since this vessel was never intended solely for claret but for any red table wine. The *wine ewer* is a grander serving vessel than the claret jug. It drew its inspiration from the classical era, being based on the Grecian urn, helmet or amphora.

Left: *A Regency claret jug cut with horizontal prisms over a band of diamonds and broad flutes above narrow basal vertical mitre flutes. With a star-cut mushroom stopper. c.1820.*

Right: *A rare Regency baluster-shaped wine ewer cut with a broad band of strawberry diamonds between horizontal prisms. With a saw-tooth rim and star-cut pedestal foot. c.1820.*

Above left: *A Georgian claret jug with three diamond-cut neck rings over a horizontal-cut band of diamonds above vertical panels of large diamonds. With a matching hollow-blown diamond-cut stopper. Probably Irish, c.1810.*

Above right: *A Georgian claret jug cut with horizontal prisms over broad shoulder flutes and a band of hobnail diamonds above narrow basal vertical mitre flutes. With a matching hollow-blown mushroom stopper cut with strawberry diamonds. c.1820.*

*A Regency straight-sided claret jug cut with horizontal hollow flutes above vertical hollow flutes. With an octagonal facet-cut mushroom stopper. c.1825.*

34

*Left: An early Victorian claret jug with a facet-cut neck ring over broad flutes, 'printies' and Gothic arches. With a matching hollow-blown spire stopper. c.1840.*

*Right: An early Victorian claret jug cut with broad flutes over deeply mitred large diamonds. With a matching hollow-blown mitre-cut stopper. c.1840.*

Unlike the claret jug, the wine ewer is almost never fitted with a stopper. *Carafe* is a French term that is used to denote merely an ordinary decanter that has never been fitted with a stopper.

Although decanters with handles had been made late in the seventeenth century by Ravenscroft, Bishopp and others, the fashion for them disappeared early in the new century. It was not until the early years of the nineteenth century that claret jugs and wine ewers began to be made. However, claret jugs from the late Georgian and Regency periods are very scarce, while wine ewers from this time are rare. All the fashionable types of cutting were used on these vessels. An exaggerated pouring lip was sometimes a characteristic feature. Handles were either plain or had their surfaces cut. A flat thumb grip was often cut at the top of the handle. In the Victorian era claret jugs might be cut, engraved or acid etched. Intaglio and rock crystal work were also used. As well as the types of handles in use earlier in the century, handles might be notched, 'teared' (hollow), ribbed or rope twisted. Engraving and acid etching were the decorative techniques most favoured on, and suited to, the more delicate and graceful appearance

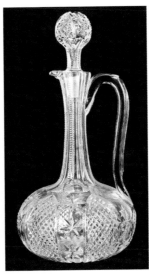

*Far left: An early Victorian claret jug cut all over with hollow oval facets. With a matching hollow-blown stopper. c.1850.*

*Left: A Victorian claret jug cut with notched broad flutes over cut large stars and diamonds. With a matching hollow-blown diamond-cut stopper. c.1880.*

Far left: *A Victorian flagon-shaped claret jug finely engraved with a bird perched on a small tree in a landscape. With a matching hollow-blown stopper engraved with foliage. c.1880.*

Left: *A Victorian ruby-cased baluster-shaped wine ewer cut with broad flutes over a polished engraving of grapes and vine leaves. With a rope-twist handle. c.1870.*

of the Victorian wine ewer. Classical motifs were often employed, such as the anthemion, key pattern or even classical scenes. These Victorian wine ewers are among the most elegant and beautiful wine vessels ever made.

Although wine ewers were usually intended for red wine, in the Victorian era ewers were occasionally made specifically for white wine or champagne. These vessels were made with a large glass pocket that

Far left: *A Victorian claret jug cut with notched broad flutes over a row of small 'printies' above a band of flat diamonds. With a matching hollow-blown stopper cut with 'printies'. c.1880.*

Left: *A Victorian amphora-shaped wine ewer etched with foliage and finely engraved with a bird. c.1865.*

Right: *A Victorian blue-cased shaft and globe carafe cut with hollow oval facets over stylised flowers and foliage in intaglio. Probably Stevens & Williams, Stourbridge, c.1890.*

Far right: *An Edwardian Art Nouveau tapered claret jug with moulded writhen ribbing. The matching hollow-blown stopper also has moulded writhen ribbing. Probably Thomas Webb & Sons, Stourbridge, c.1910.*

projected into the body of the ewer. The opening was usually situated behind the handle. The pocket is filled with ice before the ewer is filled with wine. This simple but ingenious device keeps the wine very efficiently chilled. These unusual ewers, sometimes called *ice jugs*, were often made in clear or cranberry-coloured 'ice glass', which had a rough surface resembling crushed ice. Examples made in plain glass are rare. The ice

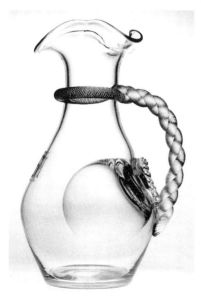

*A rare Victorian magnum-sized baluster-shaped wine ewer with an ice pocket. Decorated with an applied pincer-worked rim and a finely threaded rope-twist handle. Capacity: two and a half bottles. Capacity of the ice pocket: one pint. c.1870.*

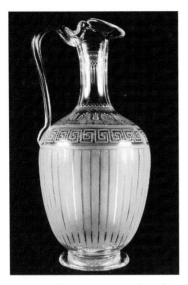

Above left: *A Victorian amphora-shaped wine ewer engraved with the dagger pattern over a band of anthemion and the Greek key pattern above vertical stripes. Richardsons, Stourbridge, c.1860.*

Above centre: *A Victorian ovoid double-cased claret jug (ruby over amber over clear glass) decorated with a polished engraving of flowers and foliage. With a matching engraved hollow-blown stopper. Stevens & Williams, Stourbridge, c.1900.*

Above right: *A Victorian magnum-sized claret jug engraved with a large dragonfly surrounded by ferns and foliage. With a matching hollow-blown stopper engraved with foliage. Capacity: two bottles. c.1880.*

Above left: *An unusual Victorian square wine ewer with canted corners and engraved with the monogram of the Earl of Craven. c.1870.*

Above right: *A Victorian baluster-shaped wine ewer finely etched with a bird, bulrushes and water plants over applied horizontal trailing representing water. Richardsons, Stourbridge, c.1870.*

Above left: *A Victorian amphora-shaped wine ewer engraved with anthemion, the Greek key pattern and pennants. c.1860.*

Above right: *A Victorian amphora-shaped wine ewer finely engraved with bands of ivy. The foot is also engraved with ivy. With a rope-twist handle. c.1860.*

pocket was not a Victorian invention but an idea inherited from the eighteenth century, when decanters had very occasionally been made with ice pockets for serving champagne. Unfortunately, despite the obvious convenience and attractive appearance of the ice jug, it does not seem to have been produced much beyond the end of the nineteenth century.

# Spirit decanters

The drinking of spirits became increasingly fashionable as the eighteenth century progressed. Although occasional examples of square spirit decanters are found from the second half of the century, most surviving spirit decanters from this time are smaller versions of the same types as those made for wine. Although they were sometimes made in clear glass, they are most frequently to be found in green, blue or amethyst glass. They

were usually produced in sets of three and often carry gilt labels for *brandy*, *rum* or *hollands*, although other spirits are sometimes encountered. Spirit decanters were often club-shaped, since they could then be fitted neatly into stands made of silver, Sheffield plate, wood or papier-mâché. Unfortunately, these stands seldom survive.

By the late eighteenth century, such was the partiality of fashionable gentlemen for spirits that they refused to be parted from them even when travelling. Accordingly, square decanters, known at the time as *spirit squares*, were made in sets of two or four, packed in specially made wooden boxes. Most square decanters were made in clear glass, although coloured examples are to be found. After 1800, the square decanter rapidly displaced all others as the typical form for spirits. They were fitted with disc, lapidary or

Above: *A rare pair of Georgian square spirit decanters with engraved labels for 'BRANDY' and 'RUM'. With original lapidary stoppers. c.1770.*

Right: *A rare set of three small Georgian plain barrel-shaped spirit decanters with target stoppers. They are shown in their original frame stand, made of wood and metal and covered with gilt-tooled red leather. c.1800.*

Above left: *A Georgian octagonal spirit decanter cut with broad flutes over horizontal prisms above a band of diamonds. With a matching hollow-blown diamond-cut ball stopper. c.1820.*

Above centre: *A pair of Regency square spirit decanters cut with prisms over plain Gothic arch panels surrounded by hobnail diamonds. The matching hollow-blown mushroom stoppers are cut with hobnail diamonds. c.1830.*

Above right: *An unusual Georgian square spirit decanter with canted corners and cut with broad shoulder flutes. The stopper is in the form of a contemporary small bucket-shaped drinking glass cut with basal broad flutes. c.1820.*

Above left: *A Georgian square spirit decanter with canted corners and cut with broad shoulder flutes over vertical mitre flutes, diamonds, diagonal mitre flutes, horizontal prisms and basal vertical mitre flutes. With a star-cut mushroom stopper. c.1810.*

Above right: *A set of three Georgian barrel-shaped spirit decanters cut with vertical and horizontal lines in imitation of the wooden staves and iron bands of a barrel. The frosted surface was produced by wheel engraving. All have their original old Sheffield silver-plated gadrooned stoppers with rope-twist ring pulls. The three labels are engraved for 'GIN', 'WHISKEY' and 'BRANDY'. c.1830.*

Left: *A rare Victorian small cylindrical ruby-trailed spirit decanter cut with flat diamonds, Gothic arches and vertical hollow flutes. With a lapidary stopper. Made by Hodgetts, Richardson & Son, Stourbridge, probably for the Paris Exhibition of 1878.*

Right: *A Victorian 'brilliant' style cylindrical spirit decanter cut with strawberry hobnails and diamonds and with a lapidary stopper. Possibly Thomas Webb & Sons, Stourbridge, c.1890.*

mushroom stoppers. On rare examples, the finial of the stopper formed the bucket-shaped bowl of a contemporary sherry or port glass. The stopper could thus be used as a small drinking glass. From the early nineteenth century, those square decanters intended for a box might have their upper portion cut with diamonds or other decoration. Those intended for ordinary domestic use might be cut all over.

In the Victorian era the proportions of the square decanter changed: tall and slim in the Georgian period, it became broader but shorter. Engraving and acid etching were rarely applied to Victorian square decanters, cutting being the preferred decoration. While all cutting patterns were used, the brilliant style was by far the most popular from the 1880s. The Victorian spirit decanter was almost invariably fitted with a large lapidary stopper, the matching stopper being a rare alternative. In the second half of the nineteenth century it became fashionable for square decanters to be fitted into a lockable frame known as a *Tantalus*. These frames were usually made of wood, such as oak or mahogany,

*A rare Victorian 'Tantalus' by Betjemanns, London, c.1880. See cover illustration and the accompanying caption on page 2 for a detailed description.*

42

Above left: *A Victorian cylindrical spirit decanter cut with the 'Russian' pattern below broad shoulder flutes. The matching hollow-blown stopper is also cut with the 'Russian' pattern. c.1890.*

Above centre: *An unusual Victorian cylindrical spirit decanter cut with broad shoulder flutes over panels containing flower heads and foliage in intaglio between circular reserves of 'brilliant' cutting. With a lapidary stopper. c.1900.*

Above right: *An unusual Edwardian Art Nouveau waisted spirit decanter with moulded writhen ribbing and a matching hollow-blown ball stopper, also with moulded writhen ribbing. c.1910.*

Above left: *An unusual pair of Victorian bell-shaped spirit decanters cut with broad shoulder flutes above large strawberry diamonds and vertical hollow flutes. With matching hollow-blown ball stoppers cut with strawberry diamonds. c.1890.*

Above right: *An Art Deco barrel-shaped spirit decanter engraved with horizontal lines. With a matching stopper. Thomas Webb & Sons, Stourbridge, c.1930.*

Above left: *An Art Deco barrel-shaped spirit decanter cut with 'printies' over stylised leaves and flutes in intaglio. With a fluted stopper. Stuart & Sons, Stourbridge, c.1930.*

Above right: *An Art Deco rectangular spirit decanter cut all over with vertical and horizontal prisms enclosing an oval reserve of flowers and foliage in intaglio. With a matching prismatic cut stopper. John Walsh Walsh, Birmingham, c.1935.*

although more expensive ones were veneered with rosewood or coramandel and could even be inlaid with marquetry. They might have brass- or silver-plated mounts. In very special examples, the frame might be entirely silver-plated and decorated all over with fine engraving. Although a Tantalus might hold from two to five decanters, most held three.

During the nineteenth century, octagonal, cylindrical or even bell-shaped decanters were sometimes made as alternatives to the square decanter. Changes in taste at the turn of the twentieth century introduced new variants, such as the hourglass shape, which might be decorated with moulded spiral ribbing. Nevertheless, the square decanter remained the traditional vessel for spirits throughout the nineteenth and twentieth centuries.

# Glossary

**Acid etching:** a technique whereby a stylus is used to draw the design through a wax coating applied to the surface of the glass. Hydrofluoric acid is then applied to the surface to etch the design into the glass.

**Amphora:** a large Greek urn-shaped jar used for storing wine.

**Annular, annulated:** a neck ring (or knop of a wine glass) consisting of three moulded ribs, giving the impression of three rings or collars combined.

**Barrel-shaped decanter:** a decanter of curved or bulbous form, resembling a barrel.

**Basal:** around the lower portion of the sides of decanters.

**Blazes:** a row of extremely fine vertical or slanted mitre cuts.

**Brilliant style:** an elaborate late Victorian style of cutting, based on straight-line mitre cuts, producing diamonds and octagonal hobnails.

**Broad flutes:** wide, flat cutting, either long or short, often applied to the neck or shoulder of decanters.

**Casing:** overlaying one or more colours of glass on another.

**Club-shaped decanter:** a decanter with broad, sloping shoulders meeting sides that taper inwards towards the base.

**Comb flutes:** narrow, vertical hollow-cut flutes.

**Cross-cut diamonds:** flat diamonds overcut with a cross.

**Cut disc stopper:** a flat, circular or teardrop-shaped stopper, often cut around the edge with lunar cuts. Eighteenth century.

**Die:** a hollow tapered drill used to grind the taper of the stopper peg.

**Façon de Venise:** French for 'in the Venetian style'.

**Fancy-shaped decanter:** a decanter with an inward-curving neck and an outward-curving body, producing an 'S'-shaped profile. There is usually a large ring at the base of the neck.

**Finial:** the decorative head or top of the stopper.

**Flagon-shaped decanter:** a decanter with its body in the form of a vertically flattened sphere.

**Gothic spire stopper:** a pointed stopper cut with facets. Eighteenth century.

**Hobnail:** an octagon produced by several intersecting mitre cuts, the top of which can be plain, cut with various kinds of star, or cross-hatched like a strawberry diamond. An important element of Victorian brilliant cutting.

**Hobnail diamonds:** flat diamonds overcut with an eight-pointed star.

**Ice glass:** glass with a specially designed roughened surface resembling crushed ice.

**Ice jug:** a large ewer with an ice pocket.

**Intaglio:** engraving performed with a specially designed cutting wheel, producing deep, crisp and polished decoration.

**Labelled decanter:** a decanter decorated with an engraved or gilt cartouche appearing to be suspended by a chain, in imitation of eighteenth-century silver wine labels.

**Lapidary stopper:** a solid ball stopper cut all over with facets.

**Lenticle:** a polished circular or oval hollow cut resembling a lens.

**Lozenge stopper:** a teardrop-shaped stopper with a bevelled edge. Eighteenth century.

**Mallet-shaped decanter:** a decanter with narrow shoulders and sides that taper outwards towards the base.

**Mitre cut:** a 'V'-shaped cut produced by cutting wheels with a 'V'- or mitre-shaped profile.

**Mushroom stopper:** a stopper with an umbrella-shaped finial resembling a mushroom.

**Nelson decanter:** a decanter with straight sloping shoulders meeting straight sides, tapering inwards towards the base. There is one ring at the base of the neck, which is usually fitted with either an octagonal mushroom stopper or a hollow-blown spire stopper.

**Peg:** the base of the stopper, which is fitted into the neck of the decanter.

**Pillar flutes:** cut convex or rounded fluting, usually vertical, resembling reeding on furniture.

**Pincer work:** decoration performed when the glass is still hot and semi-molten by using pincers to manipulate the glass into fanciful shapes.

**Pontil mark:** the scar left by separating the base of the decanter from the pontil (or punty) iron used by the glassblower to hold the piece while shaping it. The rough scar can be ground away by 'hollowing', leaving a polished hollow depression, or entirely disguised by the cutting of a large decorative star.

**Printies:** lenticles.

**Prismatic cutting:** contiguous mitre cutting, producing the sharp edge of a prism. Usually applied to an area such as the shoulder and neck or body of a decanter. Sometimes called 'step cutting'.

**Prussian decanter:** a barrel-shaped decanter.

**Quatrefoil:** divided into four lobes.

**Reamer:** a tapered drill used to shape the inside of the decanter's neck to receive the stopper.

**Regency:** strictly 1811–20, the period when George, Prince of Wales, became Prince Regent during the incapacity of his father, King George III. Since the Prince succeeded his father as King George IV in 1820, 'Regency' is usually extended to include his reign (1820–30).

**Relief diamonds:** pointed, pyramidal diamonds.

**Rock crystal engraving:** a very expensive technique used to sculpt and decorate the glass. The entire surface is polished bright to give the impression of carved rock crystal.

**Royal decanter:** a decanter of identical form to the 'Nelson' decanter except for having three neck rings.

**Russian pattern:** a particularly elaborate and expensive manifestation of the late Victorian brilliant style.

**Shaft and globe:** a decanter roughly shaped like a long-necked onion, with a narrow straight neck and a globular body.

**Slice cutting:** an eighteenth-century style of cutting that employs square-edged cutting wheels at a very shallow angle to the surface of the glass.

**Spire stopper:** a pointed hollow-blown stopper, usually cut with broad flutes. Victorian.

**Stopperer:** the glassworker whose job was to fit stoppers into decanters.

**Strawberry diamonds:** flat diamonds subdivided by fine mitre cuts into tiny diamonds, supposedly resembling the skin of a strawberry.

**Sulphide:** a ceramic cameo 'incrustation' or inclusion in glass. A cameo made of ceramic material is encased in glass and used to decorate scent bottles, goblets, bowls and decanters. A difficult and expensive process, patented by Apsley Pellatt of London in the early nineteenth century. Although his claim to the invention of the process is disputed by French glassmakers, he was certainly the first to perfect it.

**Tapered decanter:** a decanter with sides tapering gently outwards from the base of the neck to the base of the decanter without any noticeable shoulder.

**Target stopper:** a flat circular stopper cut on each side with a lenticle and bevelled around its edge. Also known as a 'bull's eye' stopper.

**Tear:** an air bubble shaped like a teardrop.

**Teared:** containing a large tear that follows the shape of the stopper, decanter handle or wine glass stem, which, in effect, are hollow-blown.

**Trefoil:** when the neck rim of the decanter is divided into three lips or lobes.

**Vesica:** a 'marquise' or boat-shaped field defined by engraved or cut borders and filled with various kinds of engraving or cutting.

# Further reading

Ash, Douglas. *How to Identify English Drinking Glasses and Decanters 1680–1830*. G. Bell & Sons, 1962.

Davis, Derek C. *English Bottles and Decanters 1650–1900*. Charles Letts & Company, 1972.

Dodsworth, Roger (editor). *British Glass Between the Wars*. Dudley Leisure Services, 1987.

Evans, Wendy; Ross, Catherine; and Werner, Alex. *Whitefriars Glass: James Powell & Sons of London*. Museum of London, 1995.

Hajdamach, C. R. *British Glass 1800–1914*. Antique Collectors' Club, 1991; reprinted 1993.

Hajdamach, C. R. *English 'Rock Crystal' Glass 1878–1925* (catalogue). Dudley Art Gallery, 1976.

Hughes, G. Bernard. *English, Scottish and Irish Table Glass from the Sixteenth Century to 1820*. Boston Book and Art Shop, 1956.

Jackson, Lesley (editor). *Whitefriars Glass: The Art of James Powell & Sons*. Richard Dennis, 1996.

Northwood II, John. *John Northwood: His Contribution to the Stourbridge Flint Glass Industry 1850–1902*. Moody & Moody Ltd, 1958.

Reynolds, Eric. *The Glass of John Walsh Walsh 1850–1951*. Richard Dennis, 1999.

Thorpe, W. A. *A History of English and Irish Glass*. The Medici Society, 1929; reprinted by The Holland Press, 1969.

Wakefield, Hugh. *Nineteenth Century British Glass*. Faber & Faber, 1961; reprinted 1982.

Warren, Phelps. *Irish Glass: The Age of Exuberance*. Faber & Faber, 1970.

Westropp, M. S. Dudley. *Irish Glass: An Account of Glass-making in Ireland from the XVIth Century to the Present Day*. Herbert Jenkins, 1920; second edition Figgis, 1978.

# Places to visit

The following are important general collections of glass containing decanters.

*Ashmolean Museum of Art and Archaeology*, Beaumont Street, Oxford OX1 2PH. Telephone: 01865 278000. Website: www.ashmol.ox.ac.uk

*Bristol City Museum and Art Gallery*, Queens Road, Bristol BS8 1RL. Telephone: 0117 922 3571. Website: www.bristol-city.gov.uk/museums

*The British Museum*, Great Russell Street, London WC1B 3DG. Telephone: 020 7636 1555. Website: www.british-museum.ac.uk

*Broadfield House Glass Museum*, Compton Drive, Kingswinford, West Midlands DY6 9NS. Telephone: 01384 812745.

*Victoria and Albert Museum*, Cromwell Road, South Kensington, London SW7 2RL. Telephone: 020 7942 2000. Website: www.vam.ac.uk

*World of Glass*, Chalon Way East, St Helens, Merseyside WA10 1BX. Telephone: 01744 22766. Website: www.worldofglass.com

*Worthing Museum and Art Gallery*, Chapel Road, Worthing, West Sussex BN11 1HP. Telephone: 01903 221140. Website: www.worthing.gov.uk

# Index